About the author

Writing is Marina-Gabrielle Cook's passion. She expresses herself through creative outlets: poetry, art and music. Artistic outlets have been her therapy through the profound emotions she emphasised in this book.

A LOVER'S JOURNEY THROUGH THE HEART AND SOUL

MARINA-GABRIELLE COOK

A LOVER'S JOURNEY THROUGH THE HEART AND SOUL

Vanguard Press

VANGUARD PAPERBACK

© Copyright 2022
Marina-Gabrielle Cook

The right of Marina-Gabrielle Cook to be identified as author of this work has been asserted by her in accordance with the Copyright, Designs and Patents Act 1988.

All Rights Reserved

No reproduction, copy or transmission of this publication may be made without written permission.
No paragraph of this publication may be reproduced, copied or transmitted save with the written permission of the publisher, or in accordance with the provisions of the Copyright Act 1956 (as amended).

Any person who commits any unauthorised act in relation to this publication may be liable to criminal prosecution and civil claims for damages.

A CIP catalogue record for this title is available from the British Library.

ISBN 978 1 80016 237 2

Vanguard Press is an imprint of
Pegasus Elliot MacKenzie Publishers Ltd.
www.pegasuspublishers.com

First Published in 2022

Vanguard Press
Sheraton House Castle Park
Cambridge England

Printed & Bound in Great Britain

Acknowledgements

I would like to thank; my family; my fiancée, Sarah; my friends, Mat, Megan and Kathy and my grade twelve English teacher, Mrs. Fretz, for always supporting my writing and encouraging me to write this book. Thank you all for helping me through this journey.

My heart is filled with piano keys and cello symphonies. Classical guitar and smooth rhythmic bars. My heart is filled with beauty and pain, sun and rain. My heart is filled with things both loud and peaceful. I just hope she finds them beautiful.

Bitter Sweet

We spend our lives trying to pick the perfect outfit, or trying to plan the perfect date. Tonight I realized we could make a cardboard fort, eat fast food in old PJs while I hold up a lighter because we're out of candles and it would be perfect. Perfect isn't an object or action, it's how I feel with you.

In French we say *tu me manques* which translates to *you are missing from me.* Isn't it beautiful to acknowledge someone is missing from you? Like that puzzle piece you've been looking for since you were eleven. You are missing from me in the Fall when the leaves paint the streets. You are missing from me when I jump through piles of leaves hoping to find peace in the smell of nature. You are missing from me when the snow starts to fall, when the air is so cold our lungs forget to breathe. You are missing from me on the days I get hot chocolate to sweeten the bitterness of winter. You are missing from me on the days I cry into my pillow wishing for the comfort of your chest. You are missing from me on most days because I could never see you enough. You are missing from me, but that's okay; if I didn't long for you, what would I ever have to look forward to?

And just like that, we became a puzzle. Our pieces fit together perfectly. My jagged edges rounded by the tides of her beauty.

I was unaware the day we met would be the start of my forever; it was my heart's secret.

The sound of her voice flipped the switch that brought me to life.

Her eyes smile and her lips welcome me like an open door.

I'd write the story of our love, but a story needs an ending.

Bring me back to life, wake me from this eternal dream, smile a light into my soul. True love's kiss didn't wake the princess; it was the radiance of a smile so pure, her eyes just had to open.

I'll spend my nights painting my love on a canvas and I'll watch the stars write a story in your eyes. A story only my lips can read. I'll listen to the wind carrying your voice in soft melodies, until every beat becomes the sound of my heart. Stay with me in this eternity of symphonies.

I never knew how powerful love could be until I realized I had fallen into the warmth of her loving embrace.

Her soft touch ignited a part of me I had forgotten existed until she reached down to the depths of my abyss to hold my hand.

I have never craved the touch of another more than when I lay in bed without your body against mine.

She leaves me speechless because saying "I love you" could never be enough to describe the eternity I see in her eyes.

The sound of her heart calms the restless tides of my mind and her every breath clears the sky.

If only every moment could be as perfect as the nights
I spend looking into her eyes.

The day I met you was the day I started living.

I'd fall apart if her arms didn't pull me back together. I'd get lost wandering the stars if I didn't hear the beat of her aching heart calling me home. I'd be blind, forever in the dark, if her smile didn't pierce the depths of every darkness. I'd lose myself if she wasn't holding my broken pieces in the safety of her palms. I wouldn't be myself if it wasn't for her.

She plays music for me every time we're together. I place my head on her chest and listen to the symphony. The resonance of her voice plays my heart like the keys of a piano. The beat of her heart hums like a cello and every breath she takes is a stroke on the violin and every laugh is accompanied by delicate fingers on a classical guitar.

She is the adventure on every map, the beauty in every sky and the wonder in my soul.

In a world we deem as dying, overwhelmed with technology, breaking our roots with nature, she is my root, my sun, and the very water that fills my cup. But, is it half empty or half full? This double sided question, does it have an answer? Does my answer make me an optimist or a pessimist? Or is this all circumstantial and opinion based? My answer, the cup is overflowing. The cup could never be anything, but full, because with her nothing could ever be empty.

Being empty implies that what is taken is never returned, but she never stops giving. No matter how much of myself I give to her, she always finds pieces of herself to trade. In the end we mix and match like a jigsaw puzzle. We are together, we are united, our souls are intertwined.

Society has no measure for perfection. Perfection is
based on perception and from every angle or view,
every laugh and smile, every breath and sigh,
perfection is the unmatched beauty behind her eyes.

She is the beauty of an unpainted canvas. Unguided our minds become vast with possibility and opportunity. White could turn into anything in moments and the beauty of chance and choices makes me wonder if we should ever paint it?

She is everything that I am and ever will be. She is my world; the very foundations I have created rest on her shoulders and my heart, my core, is resting in no place safer than her hands. The ones I trust will never hurt me, the ones I know will always comfort and hold me, right?

She was part of me. She was me in the sense that I thought I wouldn't be me without her. She was everything, and her name was love.

Everything is constantly changing and we always grow; please don't make me grow alone.

If this is to be the end, can you love me like you once did? So that in this sea of tears I may find warmth in this last bitter sweet memory.

Heartache

Please, push through the clouds of my confusion, hold me and show me there is comfort in uncertainty.

We all deserve happiness, guess it just took me awhile to realize this wasn't it.

I thought she loved me, but she only loved the idea of me. The idea of being loved the way I loved her. In the end I loved her, but she only liked me.

Nothing hurts more than when your heart is in the hands of someone who can't give you theirs.

I cannot hide from the reflections of what used to be our love under the infinite darkness of these streets.

While part of me is breaking the other is being built back up… Love has a sick sense of humor.

Pain is sometimes easier… but when it comes to love… sometimes… I'd rather feel nothing.

I cut a tree down today. Now all it was is lost in the abyss of this life. I will never again hold the joy of that tree or feel its warmth. All because the wind told me it was sick. I cut it free, saved it from despair. Am I selfish to wish I could take it back? I cut a tree down today and when it fell, so did I.

There's a broken shopping cart in the parking lot of the store where I used to work. It sits in the rain and sun, it sits under the clouds and with the stars. It basks in light and hides in the dark. Every stride gives off painful squeals. Every step closer resonates in anguish. My heart is in this cart. It couldn't move on its own any more. Now the very compass I trusted with bringing me home is lost and I don't know where to go.

Music speaks to the broken parts of me. Music reaches me in the depths of the mess you left. The high hums and low drums speak to the wailing sorrows in my chest. The slow pace and fast notes give my heart a beat… after you took way the only thing it beats for.

I've never wanted to disappear more than I do right now. Laying in this bed, crying, grabbing my head because the pain I feel right now is worse than anything I could've ever imagined.

It's on days like these I wish you could take my hand, reach inside my heart and pull away the curtain that hides me from the world.

It's been a while since I was able to write the tears in my heart. Now I find myself watching as this pen carves into this page. No longer suffering in silence, but in emptiness.

When every door shuts, when all the stars burn out and all these dreams die… that is where I will be. Left alone in the dark mess that used to be our home.

I loved you, even though I was scared to. I begged you not to hurt me. I gave you my heart and my soul; all I asked was that you leave me whole. You walked away with pieces of me I will never see again. Why couldn't you just leave me whole?

Every day when the sun sets there will be a beautiful red sky. I let my heart go and she floated up. Now she bleeds love into the sky every night, longing for warmth. A warmth I destroyed when I ended what was supposed to be our eternity.

It's lonely when you're left alone with your tears while the world's asleep.

If only expressing the hurt was as easy as letting this ink bleed on this page. The shadows in my mind, I'm haunted by my will to forget. The floods of my heart overpower this dam. Every time I close them the tides come welling back. I'm scared of drowning…

I've always had these broken pieces, but you made me forget. I never knew when you left they'd burn a hole in my chest I'll never escape. You were right when you said I couldn't know how to love you without loving myself. I'll never know how to love you right because I've never hated myself more. It's my fault I'll spend these lonely nights dancing with my demons.

Truth is… I can't dance. I cower and hide in the corners of my mind I think they can't reach. They'll always find me, even in this hole that used to hold my broken heart. I want to say I could sleep forever, but my sleep holds no dreams, only nightmares I can't face. All that's left is to suffer awake. I'll wait for the smallest sign that you're all right. Maybe I'll feel a little bit better knowing I destroyed myself more than you. Maybe it'll give me hope. Maybe I can live with this pain only if I know you're okay. I'd walk forever with this dark cloud, if only it meant you'd find the sun. I wish you'd stay, but I won't make you stand in my acid rain. I'm better off locked in this cage where I can't cause you pain. If you smile I might feel the light, so, my love, please be all right, because even from this distance your light can shine. I'm laying here blind and a second of light might save my mind.

When I walked away angry, hurt and scared, I didn't consider how you felt before I shut the door and broke our love.

If I could find the right words I'd write a novel, but my head's drowning in memories I'm trying to forget.

Oftentimes we project who we wish we were and reflect our pain and shame inside to cast it from the world and hide it from ourselves. Maybe that's why you couldn't talk to me?

We are all artists. We are born with hearts full of ink and the world is our canvas. We give and give until something snaps and we realize the beautiful world full of love took our passion and painted pain. Now our hearts are broken and as all the ink seeps out, as our joy fades, we wonder why we ever shared it.

I decided to write my feelings so I wrote "feelings" on a piece of paper and turned it into a beautiful paper airplane and threw it at my trash can. Isn't that what people do? They take your feelings, turn them into something beautiful and then throw them out like they never mattered.

What if stars were just other people looking up at the sky at three a.m., lost and looking for meaning? What if these stars are the light at the end of the tunnel I've been looking for? Or are we all just flickering lights looking for something to keep us on until we burn out? All stars burn out, some sooner than others. We never know when our lights will start to flicker. All of a sudden you find yourself amongst the sky at three a.m. looking for meaning with all the other lost souls.

"All is fair in love and war", but it isn't. Why does someone get to walk away with pieces of me while I lay broken on the ground?

The life inside of me has died. Watching it pour out reminds me this creek hasn't dried. These floods fill the empty streets of my pain. Love is a sick game, so I'll watch the red rain.

I see the eye of the storm, but I can't go into it. I've been in this hurricane for so long getting out is scarier than staying in.

Please bring my smile back. I don't think you need it any more.

New Beginning

In this rubble, the mess you've left, I see all my love shattered on the floor. As I pick up the pieces, as they start to get put back together, I realize this mirror will never be the same. These pieces will never fit together again. So here it begins, the reconstruction of myself.

The wind whispers to me through the leaves, the sun sings through the clouds and her eyes pierced through this fog and started my heart.

When I crack and my world falls, when my days blend and sleep becomes my dream, when my eyelids finally collapse in agony and exhaustion, will you still be there when I wake?

I want to pour my heart out, show you my soul. But, I'm scared of what you'd think. I'm scared of how I feel about you. I'm not always in eternal sunshine.

I almost forgot what it felt like to be alive, but then I saw you smile. In the darkness of that night sky I rediscovered my light when I kissed your lips.

I remember being lost, I wandered in an endless night for what seemed to be an eternity. Then I heard a voice. It called out to me, I followed it but I couldn't see where I was going. Everything was still dark. That's when I felt it, someone was holding me. A warmth radiated through me, and what used to be dark became beautiful. That's when I looked up and saw it was you.

There are no perfect words to describe her. Her radiance brings me the warmth of a home. Her eyes melt my every fear. Her smile ignites a fire inside me, a light in my world. Her touch makes me feel in ways I once thought only existed in fairy tales. Maybe happy endings do exist, but I'd never have enough pages to write about her endless beauty.

www.ingramcontent.com/pod-product-compliance
Lightning Source LLC
LaVergne TN
LVHW041540060526
838200LV00037B/1069